The Spiritist

TIME TRAVELERS, DEMONS, WITCHES, OUTLAW POETS AND SPIRITISTS

Theresa Gaynord

PREQUEL TO RUM RUNNERS AND PIRATE SAINTS - CLARIA - THE BIRTH OF THE DEMON FISH

Disclaimer: All names, characters and incidents portrayed in this book are fictitious. No identification with actual persons (living or deceased), places, buildings and products are intended or should be inferred.

Copyright © 2022 Impspired

ISBN: 978-1-914130-60-1

"Their screams before one last breath is taken.
That gets me off!"

OTHER TITLES BY IMPSPIRED

It's Like Walking a Tightrope –
by Mary Farrell

Particle Acceleration on Judgement Day -
By Peter Magliocco

In Between Pauses –
By Amrita Valan

Beautiful Boy –
By Joseph Mykut

Marty & Irene –
By Justin Wiggins

Old Wood Shop –
By Charlie Brice & Jim Hutt

Immersed in Blue –
By Margaret Royall

This book in its entirety is dedicated to my beautiful and loving sister, Maria Garcia (Machicha). I love you so very much!

For my family, all of my ancestral spirits and all of the inhabitants of this beautiful and vast universe, both alive and dead, real and imagined, that roam through the pages of this book.

For Matt, Mags, Maria (Machicha), Fernando and
Roberta, I love you. Thank you for always being there
for me when I needed you the most.

For my former students at Good Shepherd School in Inwood, this one's for you too.

Thank you God for always guiding my way.

Acknowledgements

Special thanks goes to Dan Hollifield and Iain Muir of Aphelion Magazine for all their love, support and professionalism. And for being the first magazine to publish my work in 2019.

Special thanks also goes to Mrs. Mary Ferrari and Sister Loretta Shanahan who were my teachers at the Academy of Mt. St. Ursula and who taught me the beauty of the written word.

I also want to thank my English professor from Fordham University, Verlyn Klinkenborg who is a non-fiction author and the former newspaper editor for the New York Times. Thank you to all my professors from the Modern Language Dept. at Fordham University for showing me how a book can not only expand your mind but take you places you could never dream of or imagine before.

I would like to dedicate this book to my mom, Elvira Margarita Garcia Alonso for always believing in me, defending me and for always being my best friend.

Machicha my sister, you were the first person to tell me all the amazing stories that sparked my imagination as a child. I love you! Thank you.

Fernando, my brother, I love you! Thank you for all your advice, guidance and love.

Blessings!

Special thanks to Arnold Cohen for being not only a wonderful family friend but someone we consider, family.

May God's love show you the way! Love to all my family members! Especially my wonderful, loving and giving husband and my heart, my awesome daughter.

Thank you Father, Son, Holy Spirit, Virgin Mother of God and All the Angels and Saints and Spirit Guides who do God's bidding especially St. Michael the Archangel and our Guardian Angels who light and guard, who rule and guide, as well as all my ancestral spirits and fur babies in Heaven for always giving my loved ones and me your continued love, guidance and protection throughout the years.

Introduction

I believe the universe is composed of both good and evil forces that are constantly and invariably intertwined, interconnected and in continual motion. In this dualistic notion, we bring that energy and consciousness into the physical world. Particles of these energies festered inside us before we even took on a human state. We may not know it but we made our choice, wrote our book even before we were born into this earthly existence. We are a compilation of everything that is, was, and will be.

Chaos in nature and intricate dualistic fury reborn into Spirit. Theresa C. Gaynord.

Contents

SPECTATORS

I gather myself collectively
even as I make my escape. The
land sees me beginning with
the smallest of creatures and
rock formations, to the largest,
increasing progressively in
surface, secured by time.

At the summit the stones show
a gentle curvature, like the
marbleized wings of a grey and
black bird. As a child I stood
here pretending to be buoyed
upward, suspended by the autumn
air.

Today my shoulders tremble,
and it is hard work to gaze
at the sun and cleave the air,
but I can still hear the sounds
of the nymphs who dwell in the
grottos and my soul gives way
to chase them without fear.

These Dryads are my partners
in dance, from the night's magick
and solitude to the daylight's
masterly manner, a regal symbol
of the universe, received
and rewarded by the goddess. Here
hand over hand, branch over branch,

of stormy teeth and claws in laden
fields of wood they dwell, time
charged by their power. When my spirit
is serene like this and the approach
of twilight is imminent, I too become
enchanted, gilded to the native fields,
out of sight, within a fleeting moment.

~

I've become the dragonfly who dwells
here, petrified in ice, set in a bed
of clear rock crystals; to the woods
I entreat my soul, promote my refuge,
secure my dignity. My story is one
of metamorphosis and I will reveal it
to you wholly, in time.

There are branches that are my sheltered
nook in fields where shape and color
labyrinth to cliffs overlooking the sea;
and what rambles on the shores are the

mutual salutations of maidens, monsters,
sea animals, gods, goddesses, and water-
nymphs.

The deities speak to me and I have learned
the power of incantations, sorted through
potent herbs, experienced nature and all
consciousness. I am the poet, with poppy
juice in the milk of her breasts. I am
the spiritist, who walks with the dead,
out of the reach of evening stars.

~

Visibility is bad today. The fog rolls
in and the woods blend with it in
disguise. It pretends to siege with
abandon a portion of this land as
if it were subduing it with force,
forgetting that there is prosperity
in hidden things, regeneration

in this wooden Trojan horse. When I
roam here my chief objective is
curiosity. I am open to the smells
of blood sunk into deep earth and
the hyacinth as it springs up awaiting
the bee's kiss. Here I take my refuge with
the spirits who feast while others sleep.

Here I am awakened with the gift of
prophesy. This is where superstition
originates, engendered by decaying
flesh that is renewed and restored into
lyre; and I can hear their sad, murmuring
symphonies. Under these conditions I offer
my predictions,

in the way of ye old traditions that unite
in the threads of life. Here in these
realms of silence, of created and uncreated
things that fill their term of life
with abodes of terror where the fog lifts
and falls through passages dark and steep,
I sense him. He will kill again.

~

In vain he seeks arguments to dissuade me,
he can hear and feel me too through the
odoriferous eucalyptus that incense, keeping
the evil at bay. His altar is not the Sun
nor the Moon that also illuminates, but the
darkness you find in the absence of both,
mouldering in the flesh of all dead things.

He is as handsome as he is fickle, dangerous
as he is charming and cunning. His disposition
is one of wit and skill that borders heaven
but does not dare enter it. So acute is his ear,

that no sounds escape him and he is as open
as I to the spittle of birds and the sensibilities
of a flower;

yet he hates the silken string that ties us all.
In a way he has forfeited the recompense that
comes from pure love, confirmed by solemn oaths
before the birthing of the universe and he does
not care that in the hierarchy of things, he ranks
lower than a demon. The runes ascertain future
events;

on the seaboard of this wild land that holds
all thoughts poetic, in sulphur pools of forest
and fire, on the grassy rims of country
serenity gleaming with beauty, swallowed by
chaotic chasms of druid magick still stern
and grim in the falling rain where my divination
is derived, I know, he will kill again.

~

And so with the wisdom I have acquired
I smite him down for now, seeking him
no further for today, he, who comes with
blackness and hermitage, he, who spills
the blood of the innocent and speaks to
me mockingly. He has put himself at the
helm of the forest and with his shield

he drinks of its waters while defiling
the spirits with his maniacal laughter.
He has not given me his name as of yet,
but those in the deep wood know it well
and when the time comes, it will be
disclosed, and his visage will be in the
open for all to see.

~

The light enters with such ease now
as the darkness is shackled far away
from me. I have the ability to do this,
to summon it up on will then redirect it
back into something positive. As I move,
my poetic intentions chronocial those
who have gone before me.

In my eyes are the phantoms of every
poet, ever author, every artist, impatient
to spill feelings and beliefs; and they
know the outwards and inwards of space
and time better than I do. They are The
Travelers; angels who have left God
to travel the universe.

There is one that comes to me often.
Flowers frame his splendid shades of hologram
light. Trees hold his posture as the
other overhead wanderers whirl and hither

in sweeping motions over planets and
constellations. He speaks to me through the
rapture of butterfly wings, and I listen…

See-er, the man you seek seeks you.
His soul is ravaged, a virus of chaos and pain
that subdues the night with conversations
of strangulation, bottling fire fires with thorny
branches of razor wire and dark fabric, so as
not to catch the light of distraction. He travels
infamously black seeking the subtlest of motions,
looking for a key that will open him up to the
mechanism of beauty once again. But his eyes
are blank, conspicuously absent, almost
spacious and yet he finds your page with all
its scrawls of inscribed ink and deciphers
you with closer scrutiny. His first attempt is
to satisfy himself as you relent to the silver
blade of his will and action, but the weight of your
soul thumps onto his chest. It startles him for a
brief second, the affinity he has found. He looks down,
unappreciative of the feeling, yet, obsessed with its
power. If you win, he will hate you, if you lose,
he will hate himself even more. The sounds of
your thoughts, your emotions, amplify echoes of
increasing panic within him, distorting his expression,
his sense of purpose. There's a protocol, a method,
a way of ingratiating yourself. The lie, that's what
makes it
fun as he walks feeling nothing. But he sees you in

himself
vanishing and reappearing in the prisms of light that
come
and go inviting him to change for the greater good and
his
eyes narrow, miserable, ready for deep scarlet; the
scent of
death, ice and sugar. He cries as he pens your name in
shadowy prose as night falls blue in the coils of Spring.

~

Flowing rain begins to fall stronger with a breeze that
settles
all around me as the traveller angel departs toward the
endless
horizon. I close my eyes and the deities dance, leaving
their
footprints on top of red, wet clayed earth.

~

HUNTING GROUNDS

I watch her from the glass window
of the bar. She's seated at the corner.
Waist long, dark hair tangle with white
silk and wisps of lingering smoke from
her cigarette. There's a delicate gesture
to the way she swerves around in the
seat, and I feel a rush of rage at her
manipulation. If a trinket is what she
desires to be then a trinket she shall
become. This one will be easy. I can
see her now, blue lips frozen, puckering
before the kiss of death. No stirring,
no eyelashes fluttering, no indication of
breathing. That's how I like my women,
cold, peering at me through empty space.

~

I walk in the Red Hook Pub. Peanuts
cover the floor wet with dirt beneath.
Shadows pass all around me, no one
ever sees me. I'm either too smooth or
too insignificant but definitely not overly
intimidating. At least not yet. Disappearing around
the corner of the stool where she sits,

my anticipation builds with sexual desire. I
want to squeeze her throat, hesitating for
just a moment to see the look of disbelief
on her face. Deceitful little sluts die, leather-
bound like the Bible I carry under my arm.
They can never believe it when death comes
for them. And I give them the option of
prayer, of crying out for help before darkness
puts an end to all their sins. "Scream!" I tell
them. "Cry out for help!" "Here, I'll help you."
"Dear God save me!" I say, mockingly,
laughing at their pain. They always plead.
They always bargain. Gutless wonders of
the world. And now this beautiful
whisky drinker, awaits me. Will she fall into my
trap?. Let the games begin. A winner has not yet
been declared. I have standards. Her sins will be
weighed and they will be measured a dozen times
before the rose is plucked from its source.
Before I make my choice.

~

The disharmony of the place edges closer to
every bartender, every waitress, every patron that
has settled there. Even the bugs that skitter around
in the darkness seem disoriented, lost in time.
Everything visible is half removed, half quivering,
startled in horror by their very existence. I can see
them

all crawling on their hands and knees, afraid.
Afraid to move, afraid to see, afraid to live. Squelching
in mud like filthy animals, fear washing over them.
Isn't it any wonder my playful laughter ignites the
emptiness of the soulless? Such easy prey, such
spineless, ravenous beasts they all are!

~

A Parisian woman, dressed in red, breasts nearly
exposed takes a seat. She's whispering strange
words to herself about chaos and the hidden pain
of a loveless marriage. She smells of incense and
carries an embroidered handkerchief with blue
flowers etched into the corners. Her hair is
strawberry blonde and her eyes are blue. And when
she walks in, the curtained windows behind me
shake with approval. There are protruding
veins on her hands, a curvy, voluptuous body now
soft to the loss of muscle mass. Nothing exists
in her anymore. No. Not her, I tell myself. Too
easy. Not enough of a challenge. I want a challenge.
I want to hear them scream. Their screams before
one last breath is taken. That gets me off.

~

The red walls of the pub resemble blood. Blooming
blood. That is why I chose this place. Here, men
masturbate in the presence of half-naked women

who disappear with the darkness. You won't find
redemption nor truth in the faces before you.
Still alive but dead inside, their whole story reads
scattered among the tuneless songs of an old
jukebox, slapped together to pacify the inebriated
faces, too hideous to look at within the twinkling dust.

~

Feeling rather smug, I peer out at the stars through
the window, holding the curtain back just a tad.
Incomparable dread fills the air. I may not find her
tonight. The dark haired woman with waist long
hair will not do. She wipes away tears while
talking on the phone to one of her children. I have
standards. She doesn't measure up. She won't
make the cut. Just as I was about to leave I saw her.
Diabolical little hussy with triumphant grin, oval
young face full of dreams, full of passion. Blond
hair cropped short to show the curve and outline of
her jawline. She is short, thin, with cfm heels that
gave her a silly gait as she walks on the peanut
shells covering the floor. What will I use on her?
I asked myself. A hammer. Bones cracking, reshaping,
blood spattering like a work of art on my clothes.
Nature retaken in the blink of an eye as roots snap
beneath her with every blow, until her bloodless
face lifts with relief. I want her to shout in horror.
I want to separate her hands, her feet, her head
from her body. I want her to plummet into earth,

petrified in the mud and grime, smothered by them.
I want us to lock eyes in bewilderment and confusion.
I want her to swallow my pain, cursed, in a limbo
state, returning the memory to the underworld.

~

She smiles at me. My living sculpture. I walk
over to her, offer to buy her a drink. Her perfume
smells like vanilla. Her eyes, honey green and almond
shaped. We talk, hold hands and grin. I'm her
knight in shining armor. She's my enthusiastic
sacrifice. My voice, soft, inviting. Her voice,
a death rattle into its embrace, into silence.
She's educated but lonely, scrambling for
companionship in the lowest of places. She hooks
her leg with mine. I don't like to be touched.
I'll gouge out her eyes, cut her legs into pieces
at lightning speed. Turn her ivory skin into a
purplish ocean.
Little wench!
She's into me. Tells me all about her trucker father
and the childhood that had her missing him all the
time. I scramble for the words, the right words to
give her comfort, healing, to gain her trust. The
lightbulbs
from the lamp above us dim even more. It chills her,
excites me. The perfect excuse to take her from the
scene. To bring her to my hunting grounds. She comes
willingly. They all do. The first blow is a light one.

I love her face, frozen in terror. She's touching her
temple, her aching head and jawline. The second blow,
her head jerks back violently. "I will tie the ropes
around
your wrists and drain your soul. You bitch!" Pieces of
teeth upon my clothes, blood stained artwork glowing,
chuckling in the midnight.

~

The trees are a restless witness and the light has faded
completely from the sky. Where have all the stars
gone? I'm
left standing there all alone. In the deeps woods, my
killing
grounds. In my head I know she sees me. In my heart I
know she feels me. She watches too, through the
visions in
her mind, like a film playing. The psychic with one eye
open,
infects me with her honor. Her pulsating soul
encompasses
all of my senses. What an incomparable force she is!
Her
punishment will be severe. She wanders outside my
range then back again.
Brings me to the brink of begging for her return. She
burns my skin
like acid, satiates my bloodlust, my want and need
leaving me helpless.

Shower of Sparks

This is not my breath, it's his. The bodies are
dancing
before me, marching in a macabre procession, no
longer
hidden in the wood. He kills again and again and I
see him
do it, through shades of blues and greens,
magnified in
the shadows where dawn is a distant glow, a myth
that is never realized. How this all began is a story
unto
itself. When the electrical sparks jolted and the
standoff
between good and evil clutched both our hands
seizing
us in their acidic presence, our souls, frozen to the
ice of
time. It was on a Sunday afternoon, when the
sister of one
of the victims appeared before me at my spiritual
shop
looking for guidance, solace, a reading. Inside my

tea

room, my reading room, purple iridescents
sparkled

in the darkness from the lava lamp, positioned in
the altar

to Eleggua. Pain gripped my stomach, gouged at
my heart,

the minute I began the channeling. Her light
flickered

before me, and I suddenly saw his face, contorted,
possessed

and then her form, fading before a gauzy blade. It
was then

that the monster poisoned its astral body into
mine in an

abomination that would link us two until the end
of time.

A snake with two heads, one good one evil, ripple,
slither

in unison, one paying witness to the other,
beneath the wings

of blowing storms, infinitely resounding in
presence, in force.

~

Midnight Arrows

The Lenni-Lenape still roam these parts. I hear their calls
in the deep woods, Men of Men, Original People. They
are the grandfathers, the ancients ones, who still roam
among dandelions and scented flowers, sealing the
sacred
space with low nasal chants while drumming in the
divine home.
The sun's horizon interrupts morning incantations,
rituals
silent, secret, that twist around the smoke of peace
pipes
dancing in the air. The spirits, ghosts, sprites and
deities,
whisper to one another within the sweet symphony of
all
past things. Matrilineal clans gather, clearing the fields,
building houses with sigils of protection. With beaver
pelts and bear skin mantles, they still live among the
fog,
watching silently. Their spirits gliding, suspended,
glowing
with the fireflies in midair. Entangled in all this is the
mosaic
of myself, hidden, yet, walking among them too. We

are a part
of one another, interconnected, yet, scattered through
time.
Their fiery auras spin around me, collapsing in the hills
among rambling branches through small breaks of
bittersweet
rain in the distance.

~

Dancing Patrons

It's country music night at the Red Hook Pub.
There's an endless circle of cliques in every
direction, standing around, talking, intrigued
with anticipation at the night's intensity and
promise. Eyes lock in seduction waiting for
the introduction, for anyone to identify
themselves among the surface inquiries and
fake smiles. I'm there too. Among the masses of
humanity, looking for my chance with that
special one from within the crowd. I move among
them, with them, they welcome me with open
arms. I'm liked, trusted by the fools dancing around
the clock in a pathetic display of simple mating rituals.
But she's in my head, observing, begging me to
stop and repent. I feel her among dancing, shifting
feet, and the details of her sympathy for me are not
forthcoming. I see her sob in my mind's eye, not
so much for the victims, but for me. Lights fade
like a ritualistic ceremony and the pub becomes
pitch black. I experience the collective sound of wind,
and mingling feet. And in my sadness I search for her,
for the seer that holds my soul and my heart in her
hands.

~

Shimmering Violet

The moon's rays are casting purple wisps of eerie
mists all around it. Tonight I await my love, a
captain in the police department. I can control my
gift of sight at will and tonight all I want to see are
the eyes of the man whose gaze takes me on a
journey to a violet lake where covered bridges
hold
the secrets of our words, our love, our feelings for
one another, willing to make any sacrifice. The sky
holds whispering untold secrets that lay deep
within
our bones. This is where he holds me tight, where
his
caresses are hallucinogenic and where our love
making
can fade together into oblivion.

~

Midnight Bonfires

Witches walk the deep wood tonight, a coven
born of Osiris. Bottles of old rum and athame
to cast a spell, summon the dead. The faint red
glow of a bonfire ignites the spoken word
of magick as the high priest makes his offering.
A grimoire sits contained within the ruins of
rocks and infiltrating grass. By the river's edge
a solitary hooded figure stands in the shallows,
waist deep, peering out into the darkness. She looks
at the stars above, glows within the murk like a
goddess. The wind whips around her, everyone takes
a deep breath. Osiris warns them about her with
screeching crows as the conjured spectral apparition
of Isis explodes with energy, interfering with nature
itself. Thunder roars, lightning strikes a tree as
rain and hail begin to fall. The coven scatters, runs in
fear,
while the grimoire is left behind to melt among
obsidian cries and blue electricity.

~

Ingenuity

I feel his presence just for a moment before
the sun rises on the horizon. Insomnia operates
like a medicine bottle made of glass, empty,
lying on its side. My eye sockets look around
the room. My love sleeps soundly beside me.
I watch him hungrily, yet, like a docile child,
succumbing to his wants and needs. He moves
around in bed, stretches while opening his eyes.
A vacant smile until he holds me in his arms. He
falls back into slumber immediately and I feel
something is amiss. White-hot pain bursts across
my chest. The heaviness takes my breath away,
makes me sick to my stomach. I worry about
my love dying on the job. I fear the hideous
predators of the day and night all around him.
Trembling, I lose myself in his arms within the
privacy of his touch. Even the tentacles of the demons
that roam all around us, respect the moment, until
his Scottish accent and mild voice bids me a fond
farewell for the day; until we meet again within
the normalcy of our lives.

Cigar Rings

The precinct smells of Cuban cigars. Detectives
gather together, opening windows to release the
tobacco-fug as cigar rings smoke in circles from
the mouths that chatter and laugh in unison.
Cramped conditions give way to a conglomerate
of essences that waft through humid air. There
are arguments, raised voices about the cases each
are working on. Others examine the slightest of
clues, quietly, sullenly without distraction. Bloodshot
eyes jitter around piles of files stacked high in
disorder.
In the interview room, protocols are followed while
the answers to questions take on a patronizing tone.
Flies swarm over left over food, half-eaten and
abandoned in open Styrofoam containers. In the
middle of the room, a bulletin board holds the pictures
of the missing women among the beats of taps
from shoes and hard-nosed brass. Some gaze while
others pass on but the Captain hesitates with a look
of recognition while the posted faces stare at him in
horror.

~

Somnambulists

The aroma of pungent spices
fills my kitchen as I clumsily
make morning coffee and
samosas at 3am. The Hindu
gods and goddesses watch me
as jasmine incense permeates
in air. The house is clean, my
bed is bare, and sleep has not
come for me this evening.
Beyond words are anxious
thoughts, darting in and out
of my conscious mind. The
killings have stopped as have the
visions, a sort of balance restored
but for a moment. And like a
punch to the gut I grip myself
from across the table knowing full
well it's not over. His gaze still holds
mine in the shadows. I see the folds,
the curve of the rocks and I relent
to him, the killer, the enforcer of
a reality that drains purity from all
good things. He takes liberties and
seizes power and control that do
not belong to him. The nature spirits

grow restless for that is their domain.
His punishment will be severe. I
wonder about the identity of this man
who takes my sleep from me and the
contempt he has for all the forces of
the universe. Even when things are
calm, quiet, still, yet, wide awake.

~

Paper Birds

A kite flies, soars high in the atmosphere.
The evocative contrast of sky and light
through the surface of painted paper-
birds radiates a surreal quality, like that
of floating lanterns over waves of water.
Silk curves fold and uncurl amidst winds
that steady them higher, so close they appear
burning by the sun. In the distance the
smell of charred wood appears and disappears
with the kites' travels. Little boy maneuvers,
performs with his dad. The wood is alive
with life as the illusionist plays running down
the park's paths, adamant about flying. There
are pale roses, blades of tall green grass,
dandelions to blow and make a wish on.
Skywriting from planes up above proclaiming
mechanical handwriting perfectly structured
to compete with cascading waterfalls and
twisted vines suddenly appear. Stumbling
forward, little boy closes his eyes before
hitting the ground.
His father looks down, picks the child up in
his arms so he doesn't see the fingers raking
up from the severed arm beneath the soil.
The motion of the paper birds ceases instantly,

collapses to the ground, as the winds shift and drift toward the endless horizon.

~

Twisted Fingers

The detectives retrieve the body parts,
withered, pale, lifeless, including the
decapitated head. Loosened rocks fall,
hit the ground hard with the disturbance.
The scratch of pen on paper, jostling.
The wood, obliterated as more and more
bodies turn up, moulded around
wooden piles and soil. An ensemble
among playing children, hikers,
and the handlebars of an old, red, discarded
bike, where menacing whispers bubble
against the vacuum of fresh, dry air.

~

Falling Rain

There is a way conflict and gravity
affect the tidal estuary of the
nearby river that is highly intriguing.
In the course of dreams there are
tricky things like this. I look at the
waves infused with strange magic,
with enough vitality to endure but I
am not impressed by them. The
currents hold the darkest of moments,
details of dark winds, debris, and
consumption. I often cast spells by
the river's edge, my body immune
to falling rain.

~

Slivers

There is a long scream that no one hears by the river's edge. A scream sealed within its own disobedience. Slivers of glass protrude from her eyes as blood travels down a pathway into oblivion. I glance at my creation and smile. I did this! My gait is slow and steady. I never stress. I have peculiarities like this, but I'm not haunted by ghostly sounds. Even she doesn't rattle me anymore. I've got her under control. The nature spirits that reside here will tell her about my latest kill. And she will feel me as I do her, with bloody trails and stench emanating from my very soul. I am the demon she cannot control. I am the demon in the inferno of the human mind, crouched in the shadows. I am the sociopath that smiles at foolish adversaries. I am the secret preparing your eyes for my lover's touch.

~

Fine Competitor

There's an alien race of paranormal
beings fighting against one another.
One, with puma eyes glowing like
fire shows his long fangs, hungry
for the kill. The shapeshifter walks
with the demon, side by side, in
absolute fury, peering his long muzzle
at the vampire, diseased and pale, also
walking the wood along the river,
searching for prey. Dimensions cross
the regions of reality, all traitors to
human hands working for the good
of mankind. Tinged with the bitterness
and ruin in the absence of light, they
each yearn for the melancholy happiness
that evades them, shuts them out,
rejecting and condemning them to the
utter labyrinth of the universe, forever
lost and wanting. Time keys float
backwards in deep space, unlocking
visitors, transients, both good and
evil , all fine competitors, strewn and
scattered in a cosmic display where
the eternal struggle gives credence

to all discarded galaxies suspended
among the semblance of life and
death.

~

Beneath Journal Pages

She was cold and I could feel the shivers
pass through her body before he killed her.
In my journal I draw the seal of Solomon.
The talisman protects me against such
aggressive visions. Sometimes I feel
like a dying insect, writhing in pain, alarmed
and motionless, frozen like a dragonfly
in ice beneath the roar and fury of a huge
storm; collapsed onto my side, still.
Atoms of pure energy course through the
moonlight in a lightning surge as all evil
howls, pacing in the wake of nightfall.
Terror radiates, hackles like the thorns on a
rose. The snake slithers and raises its head,
its body, into a hunting position as creatures
pant with approval. Spirits dance with the consent
of all spectres, deities, nature spirits, angels, faeries,
and demons, as free will encompasses without
judgement, to the temple of morning light.
The stars twinkle against velvet blackness,
leaving their mark on the rivers' waters.
Across empty roads is the deafening sound
of silence, bound either to a dream or a
nightmare. We are legends, sustained within

the rise and fall of the universe, fighting
to inherit earth, battling for a space beneath
these journal pages.

~

Black Branches

As a child I swung on black branches.
Their limbs flowed with pure and simple
joy. Even when some cracked and I
fell to the ground, the challenge was
unexpected fun. In the winter months
a white blanket of snow covered them,
but I still played in the hollows, picking
up fallen logs, spinning round wildly
into my sacred space, watching the
steam pour from my mouth as I laughed
at the glimmer on the surface of snow.
It looked like a thousand tiny stars!
Orbs scattered around me, pearly,
souls of the departed, ancestral spirits,
floating beside me, watching, guarding,
and playing along. I seek to find those
memories today, to call them back up,
to resurrect them, in the wake of sleepy
eyes that dispel the fear.

~

Drops Of Blood

He almost kills again but something
holds him back. His breath grows erratic
as he creeps over to the bathroom mirror.
Drops of bright red blood pour from his
nostrils. The morning brings quiet, becomes
a whisper to the torture that hides the
dead. What if he ceases to exist? What
if he were erased, forbidden to lurk among
the living? He scrambles anxiously
for a towel to catch and halt the drops of
blood. Crimson to the absence of love, of
life. He doesn't believe in goodness
or miracles or mis-aligned emotions
that will steer him wrong. He could lose
control at this very second, blow someone's
brains out in the blink of an eye and shudder
at the two personalities within; one with
a soul, the other without, haunted into a
fiery silence that breeds drops of pure, red
blood.

~

White Gloves

White gloves hover over man's blood,
dancing suspended in the dark; glinting
an illuminating eerie blue-light, swaying,
crawling, waving hello. White gloves
dangle waiting to be yanked, waiting to
be slipped by fingertips pulling at the
silken weave of white fibers, sprinkled
red by the splashing of warm blood all
around them. White gloves cover and
conceal the howling winds that bring
about a heartless crimson moon.

~

Applause

The captain stretches his fingers
across long metal tables, moving
from one to the next, occupied by
blueprints and sketches that have
traversed the shelves of the precinct.
Details, figures, wait patiently
like timepieces, housing fears and
legends amongst the deceased. He
commits them all to memory, inscribing
each one in his mind, asking
questions, examining the technical
aspects of the killings. Hands glide
to the proper time, to the proper
space as the planets align in a macabre
dance that spins the hands of a clock
into place. A slow, steady tick-tock
begins within the heavy weight of
applause, not a clue, not a opening
as the curve of fingers gravitate toward
the other, not touching, not moving
just the same, like the curved up
smile on the face of someone
who understands the rules,
completely independent from their
opponent.

Residue

A cup of tea leaves residue,
weathered under porcelain,
attached to the bottom and sides
in an intricate pattern only a
Romani can decipher. Obliterated
emotions are kept hidden, as hope
flutters under her gaze, pushing
on glass, threatening to enter her
sacred space. Sounds reverberate
as the peering begins, a scratch of
pen on paper, the jostling of
automatic writing, the smell of
earth and rubber intertwine.
There's intestinal gurgling, something
climbing inside, pushing its way out.
Simulated movements among the
tea leaves interact with synchronicity
as glances position them with the
power of divination. Partly strewn
a face emerges, like a photograph,
that darkens the morning sky. The
telltale gaze of her eyes widen.
There are tiny pinpricks of colored lights
somersaulting before her as the Romani
spits into a crystal ashtray, aware

very aware of who the killer is. A
graze of red lipstick on porcelain
where tea leaves have molded into
place, leaves its mark. A preferred
chaos before the unveiling.

~

Running On Empty

I am not afraid of the boogeyman,
I am a boogeyman. I am not
of this earth nor this time, I travel
open portals between parallel universes
appropriating bodies, sending subliminal
messages to weak minds that do my bidding.
I am the infinite, wandering from one
reality to the next. I dwell in dreams
so ghastly, ready to slit a throat or two
or three. I am the slightest provocation,
the reason that makes you shudder with
fear, the moment of trust that cannot
be undone. I am real anger, real hate,
the new version of an old lover that
makes you hallucinate true love. I
am that petulant whisper you cannot ignore,
the fiddler of days of old. I know
you well.
I am not afraid of the boogeyman, I am
the boogeyman. And now, you know me.

~

Aflame

I am the breath aflame within
the body of a spiritist. Twigs
and twine speak to me among
the mid-squawk of birds. I am
the lightbringer who regenerates
the bones beneath the ground, the
master of your apocalyptic vision,
the small gesture of magick that
outlines blades of grass, marking
them with man's mortality. I am
the smoldering pinks, the gentle
grays in the horizon receptive
to the return of beauty. I am
the formula of relevance you
cannot ignore, the cohesive energy,
integrated, silent, that dismantles
your defenses, shattering the walls
of self-protection that leaves you
vulnerable to my mission. You
are the vision I see in my rituals,
the divination exposing the apex
of love against the coldness of winter.
You are the Earth, extended in spirals,
unreachable, barely hanging on. I
am the spiritist who captures the joy

and sorrow in the milk of her breasts,
the one who feeds the universe with
her love. The cell memory you can never
destroy. I am the writer that understands
the nature of your poetry, the one who
now can see your face and knows your name.
You are the killer, the demon exposed, the
darkness which looms between drops of
rain. And I know you. Tonight,
in the stillness of sleep, I will end your reign
of terror. I am aflame within cerulean skies.
I see you and I know you see me.

~

End Game

A simple metal trolly construction,
houses a savory meal. The cart
itself, covered with photographs
of fast food combinations. There's
a trademark umbrella opaque to
smoky air as it hovers over the stand.
The captain stalks it before he approaches
with money in hand. One hot dog,
mustard, onions and a root beer;
scraps given, tossed to a stray mutt
as it stares up in bewilderment at
the kindness. In a nearby restaurant
a cook hauls a pile of trash while
minutes drag on. In the burial-ground,
there is silence. The captain walks
passed street performers playing
brass drums. A blast of light from
the vibrations of thunder far off in
the distance follow his every step,
without a drop of rain.

~

Perfectly straight white teeth glisten
with saliva and he can hear his own
heartbeat as he hunts his next
victim. The sounds from the Red Hook
Pub grow louder and louder, its
momentum feeding the mind, churning
gears of obsessive malice, scrambling
in the surrounding darkness. Jazz music
snakes through the property. Guitar,
bass, drums, a trumpet and sax
accompany an old piano. The raspiness
of a man's singing voice breaks noise,
skips between bare legs dancing
to the smooth beat.

A snap.

The knuckles of a man's hands
intervene as the spotlight catches
a glimpse of his face. The light
washes over the sweat of his
forehead, photocopying
every wrinkle while nostrils
flare in unison with a wicked
smile.

~

You could breathe the aroma
of thunder without rain,
the fire in the sky and the
dryness of the grass. The
screams and gasps appropriate
for the night's surrender.

~

Blood runs, cruises and slithers
from a disemboweled body.
The voice of a man, embodying
that of a scared little boy, bellows
falsettos with a sinister giggle.
"Mmmm, oh, you're such a flirt!"
He scrapes the knife blade across
stone. "Honey pie!" The river's edge
glows eerily, sloshing back and forth,
violently. A sweet smell emerges,
something familiar, revolving around
the adrenaline of the night. The sounds;
twigs breaking drift past the killer,
reminds him of the spirits of the dead.
He tinkers a few minutes with the knife,
before letting out a cold laugh that echoes
from the darkness above and below.
The spiritist emerges from the bushes,
locking eyes with the killer, as if all
darkness suddenly vanished, as if they
were standing on neutral ground.

~

He freezes at her presence. As if his reputation
for being a bloodthirsty monster had all but
vanished, releasing the beast into the woods
without the use of torches or pointed sticks;
uncomfortable in the limelight. Fifty-two
deaths, all mutilations, and she looks at him
with pity.

~

"No no no! Why did you follow me?"
His tone made his agony obvious.
The Captain's mouth explodes open,
spitting out a wall of vomit and water,
as if he'd almost drowned in the
river, yet saved by some unseen force.

~

"I know my fate as I know yours."
The spiritist stands her ground,
as if anchored to the earth by a
maelstrom of good and evil forces
smoldering her down through a
swirl of mist and fog. She sucks
in her breath, holds back tears
as she sees the corpse on the ground
by his feet.

~

"Look at you, you've soiled your wedding dress."
He sings the words, madly unraveling, as if
already condemned and cast into eternal
darkness. A flock of seagulls are heard
in the distance stirring around red and blue
neon lights. You could sniff
the fishiness of the water, the pollution.
"I've cried in my sleep, buried my head
in the sight of rainbows, held my secret,
with courage! I am the man, dressed in black,
dawning the upside down crucifix in the
upstairs space of your consciousness. The
thoughtless devil whose page you cannot turn!"
A strong wind pushes between trees in the thickness
of the woods. The final battle lines have
been drawn. There's an awful dread,
the sound of running feet, then ripping flesh.
A coyote howls as a tree branch drifts
across flowing waters.

~

Abandon -The Bird Man

The Bird Man feeds the pigeons in
that little space by the Opera House
where advertising billboards lay smashed
and drunkards shout out to one another
about nothing at all. Everything turns,
even the love a little girl has for a doll,
now discarded among bird feces and
beer bottles, where cyclists ride by
without taking any notice at all. The city
hides secrets even the sun would never
dare reveal. The birds scatter as the noise
of a police helicopter drifts overhead.
The BirdMan is gifted in the sixth sense,
he knows the agitation, the chopping
its blades can bring. He's been alone on
the street, deciphering every alarm,
every siren, every horn most of his life.
He once listened to L'abandon d'Ariane Op. 98,
and decided to name himself Abandon-
The BirdMan. He was bitten by a snake once;
said the beast looked almost eight feet tall,
and gave him visionary powers, hoodoo, in the
wake of all things spiritual. Terror radiates
like a drug and comes in many forms. But
power, it courses through veins, makes
you immune to its claws and talons. The

BirdMan often repays the gift of that
snakebite, the debt, with a blood sacrifice.
And the pigeons, well, they still flock to him
in abandon, afraid of the solitude themselves.

~

SUNSETS

I've always asked myself questions during
sunsets. If the answer did not occur to me in
ten seconds then I had my answer. Sunsets
timelapse in just ten seconds as if they were
swallowed whole and hard by the Earth,
an attempt at regaining composure. Vengeance
runs cold in one long moment where
everything liquifies as your soul splits in two.
I am the spiritist that bows to the five-pointed
star projected symbolically in the horizon. I
am in uniformity with the universe that
hangs suspended, tilting back and forth,
spinning like a crazy merry go round in
darkness, still expanding, as stars and
galaxies float farther away all the time.
Beneath my feet is a apocalyptic prison,
where strange creatures dance on keyboards
morphing tones that mutate into symphonies
of death. I am the dragonfly who dwells
here, petrified in ice, set in a bed
of clear rock crystals; I am the spiritist,
that familiar material of the universe
composed of protons, neutrons and electrons.
I am the spiritist, gilded to the infinite and
filled with both darkness and light.
~

Wordless Bliss

I'm left in silence. In nothingness.
Stupid, stupid nothingness. Sometimes
you find that the darkness within you
leaves you nice and quiet even though
hungry ghosts still stir and you stare up
as her eyes meet yours. I don't like
this game anymore. I can smell my own
burned ashes and urine, bouncing between
the shadows on the bare walls of hell.
There are volumes of poetry filled with folklore.
I roam the pages of those books. Even though
most have faded with the dusk, inked
in fortunes that foretell the future. It's
a small city, when you walk it alone
in companionable silence. Tell me,
do you have sympathy for the devil?
Do you?

~

Voodoo Shop

Black smoke billows from an incense holder,
some strange combination of patchouli and myrrh.
Celebratory music plays in the background, while
a Rottweiler snores from an adjacent room. Under
a constant purple, electric light, the statue of Hecate
radiates with an incandescent glow. Deliberate
eyes watch, follow from behind the counter. It's
the illusion of freedom.
Chants accompany the drums, monitored by the
blood pressure and heart rate of willing participants.
Bone curtains billow from the frantic rush of
sudden energy in sacred space. There's a scowl
on the high-priestess's face. She doesn't like
strangers. Several dead entities roar from inside
of her, roughing and wetting her black skin.
Before the Earth, before the sun, particles
of time burst and festered inside beings
not quite born into their human state. And the
priestess, well, she's the primeval ocean;
primitive, instinctual and raw. The spiritist.
The repeater. The conduit between parallel
universes set in time, wandering from one reality
to the next.

~

A perfumed and sensual maze of corridors
fills the Voodoo shop upon galleries of
ancestral portraits that echo like a kiss in
the wind without a future, without purpose,
without a sense of place. Blessed idols
bring you favors, within favors, as offerings
scatter in abundance. You can wander, you can
watch and pace peering into the darkest nooks.
You can even taste or allow yourself to be
possessed staring stoically, half gone, unwavering
to the others gazes, also disengaged from the
material world. Whispers come from different voices,
unsettling the subtleness of an afternoon.
Honey jars attract disoriented flies, moving
and falling in horizontal lines. A promise
from the loas that money is to come. The
Voodoo shop doesn't judge, doesn't condemn,
doesn't discriminate. It's as thick-tongued
and muddy as the vibrations around her. It's
the portal, the beating heart of the netherworld.

~

Hoodoo Conjurers

Bluish light glows from an old tv
with extended antenna. A hospitality
sign hangs half in, half off in
the room of a small shack. A
child watching cartoons pops a
soda can open. Empty chairs and
a chain curtain separate the dwelling
space. In the garage, metalwork
is taking place. Souls wander,
scurrying around, lost with
incomparable force. Steaming
breaths, rancid with dried blood
and decay watch in silence, reaching
out with spectral fingers. In a cellar
where innumerable wooden boxes
are stacked, conjurers clap their
hands together, chanting among
blood curdling screams, incantations
that summon the dead. Drums call
an evil horde of deities as medicine
makers work on healing spells amidst
nauseating stenches. A goat faced beast
half man, half animal appears in the cold
pit, harrowed over the noise and urgent
calling while golden beings stand guard

ready for the fight. Down the wide
dirt road, the spiritist walks looking
for something to identify with. Her
melodious approach increasing the
tempo of the drums. Steep hills rise
giving way to other steep hills as the
path snakes around sharp bends. From
the depth of his soul the Captain can
feel her imminent approach. In his
space there is an old secretary, so
large it seems to be touching
the ceiling. Clenched fists, awkward
enough to show frustration, shakily
open the desk drawer. The skeleton
key jams before the unlocking. There's
an awful chill that comes and goes with
each passing second. And the gun,
well, its sound is familiar against
the broken equilibrium of metal
splintering slimy chunks of skull,
of brain, saturated by the power of
revenge
and
retribution.

~

The Demoning

There are monsters that walk many mansions
urged to inundate the material screen of
this world. Wispy fingers scratch at
skin, tearing flesh in the quietness of an
early hour. Giant squid like creatures with
tentacles and bloodshot eyes suck plasma
from the purest of souls with no other
intention than to leave them dry, withered
and exposed. Somber and pale faces shuffle
backwards, dressed all in black, an attempt
to repel any negative energy. Shape-shifters
dawn wings cursing the fiddler's song that
lances back and forth brutally between
half bricked walls. And I the beast unwounded
with scaly skin and puckered red lips walk
among them. I am the other narrator that
roams through the pages of this book, the one
who stalks you, draws you in, writes
your name in the fiery flames. I am the one
that spins the web, controls your dreams,
kisses your imagination under velvet sheets,
building your fanciful world bit by bit.
 I am the matrix,
the cornucopia of illusion, built from blood
and sorrow, that enslaves you, leading you

further and further away from the truth. Everything
from my creation falls apart, passes with time.
Tell me, do you nervously await your turn?
I know your names. And I welcome you with
open arms. You think you can escape, how
very quaint. They're here with me too. The
Spiritist and The Captain. They both have
fallen but the violin has skirled on. If you
listen carefully, you can hear its melodious
tune.

~

Beneath a black moon cratered by explosions of fire,
particles of nebula platoon over red plains as distant
worlds pass one another at lightning speed. Through
the ripples of this warp, a man whistles in
contradictory
song, panicking the fiddler whose playing has
miraculously
come to a halt. Crashing suns explode on either side, as
he
walks between the portals of universes, wandering
from one reality to the next, looking for his love,
looking for more sacrifices. Demons far and wide bow
to him in honor, all the while hating him for that
relinquishment of power.

~

Touching snakes spit out venom as they slither passed
tiny bursts of fire, erupting randomly, smoldering
on and off, stronger and steadier with wild vibrations
that resemble a carnival game. Swirls of mist and
smoke
curve into a funnel, like a dim light around the tunnel
of a black hole. The Captain stands with eyes
transfixed
into a hungry stare, expelling the cursed and defeated
demons from his sight for all eternity. He sees her on
the other side, The Spiritist, the one who liquefies
his soul, entangles his senses. He can't cross over,
he can no longer touch her. Not even a bargain with
the Devil himself will crack the mirror of truth. He's
lost her. Spinning blades close in, ripping through
flashes of white, enhancing the darkness.

~

Spinning waters churn, a baby emerges from blood
streaked thighs. The first cry, the trashing body,
wounded from small squeals and shrieks; the pain of
cold
air into tiny lungs. Several breaths are taken, and the
crackling flames burn as he watches her rebirth.
Terror seizes his heart, his ears strain from the sound
of silence. His body shakes. He contorts his mouth
full of pain, full of sorrow . A rock of fire the size of

a basketball floats passed him, shooting off like a
rocket, far away into empty space. The force sucks
him back, pulls him away, and he cries deep sobs,
turning all into acid rain.

~

A thick cloud of birds screech in the darkness
as demons far and wide fly in wild circles
running into each other in reckless abandon.
Archers with flamed bows and arrows take
pot shots, killing some in mid flight. Chaos
camouflages order, spinning the wheels
of fate as devil hooves thunder loud and
nasty against dried red dirt. Rows of spectators,
satyrs, time travelers, demons, witches,
outlaw poets and spiritists dance in place,
like puppets on strings on top a half-mooned
hill, condemned to awed silence.

~

Angels Among Us

A golden film of cobwebs
float delicately in air, a fabric
born of love, caches far off
in the distance, leading the
white moon in a dance that
rumbles slowly, growing louder
as it descends, sweeping over
you, over me before ascending
back to the mountains of your
mind's eye. Spirits elevate, glimmer
within the joy, releasing immortal
harmonies, clinging to souls, before
falling asleep in exhaustion.
Traces of lives well lived, regenerate
like a single glowing marker
released back into the universe,
saturated in light. Details
process as the door swings open,
transforming everything into a
preferred balance; everything
into its appointed
time.
All creatures, small and large,
are a part of the whole, even
witches, ghouls, time travellers,

demons, outlaw poets and spiritists,
have their place within the process.
Electrical spins, invisible claws
splinter in air as angels whisper,
ringing chapel bells while the faithful
carol in the streets below.
The universe blurs, silhouettes,
eviscerating the darkness for
ten seconds while cosmic
nightmares hold their sinister
grins and Alien kingdoms
do their part tempting fate,
as space and time bend
into the echoing night.

~

Heavenly angels walk among
graves, while lantern lights
glow on and off imprinting the
scene without any paranormal
explanation for the resurrection
of the dead. The manifestation
unearths ghouls that consume
the human flesh of those
recently buried who didn't quite
make the cut, but who were
instead condemned to malicious,
malevolent darkness. White
witches, spiritists and light

bringers intertwine with angels,
an unexplained supernatural
occurrence against the black
magic of devils, demons,
werewolves and vampires that
watch with skepticism and
resentment at the non-inclusion.
Slight scatterings of damp earth
footprint, as the rusted hinges of
an iron gate open just a tad across
settling earth mounds.
Good and evil pulsate steadily
in unison among the mundane
realities of everyday life and death,
among every sunrise and sunset
where creatures shiver and gusts
of winds whistle, whipping
bare branches without remorse.
Through the screen of a black
and white tv, static portals a room
in a faraway land, in a place where
your future can be foretold for only
ten dollars, where the mysteries
of the universe can become a
flourishing business, in a land of
kill
or
be
killed.

~

Guardian angels watch as a child
sleeps in her crib. Debris falls in a
courtyard from an oncoming storm
as the sky turns an ominous
red-pink. The baby seems delighted
by all the activity. Her blanket ripples
a bit even though the room is secure
from any breeze. And the child with wide grin,
arms spread
apart,
flailing,
seems to be responding to Mother Nature's
precarious spectacle, with welcoming arms,
sealing her fate once again
as
the conduit,
the immortal,
the spiritist,
who walks symbolically,
between many mansions.

~

STILL WATERS CHURN

Gale force winds and water start to inundate roads, billowing
violently over bridges, pervading the Valley of Vinales as if
summoned to complete a specific task. There are murmurs
muttered in exasperation, desperate hands gathered around
a half a dozen breeding tanks occupying the lush gardens
of a government-funded estate. The water levels in the pools
rise faster, and the quest to drain them becomes like a puzzle
or twisted game.
Brackish water continues to slosh over its edges, overflowing
onto the cobblestone walkways that are littered with glossy
green leaves and orange blossoms. First glance at the nearest
breeding tank, surrounded by purple jacaranda,
creates panic.
The Claria are escaping. Their unique form of locomotion

is unmistakable. With a preternatural sense they head for the
jungle that borders the property… for the river system that lays
beyond.
Only those involved will bless themselves and Cuba against
the terror the hurricane has just unleashed. Only those
involved will appreciate this very personal message, from
Mother Nature herself!

~

The next day the sun is shining like an oracle
in the sky. Fingers of intermittent light follow movement,
penetrating the depths of murky waters. In the shallows
where the lilies are thick, a female Claria sloshes about like
a serpent, looking for food. The sky settles down on the
earth as the clouds dissipate in heated air. All is calm.
Loneliness does not fail to induce a rush of hormones
that fuels her hunger. A burst of speed, jaws open,
a brief struggle; the end of a silvery tilapia's life. And
in the shallows, amid the vegetation, a clutch of tilapia
eggs meet the same fate. She dines on them like the
queen that she is.

Loneliness.
Her family is scattered throughout the myriad
of waterways that lace the countryside. She longs to be
with her own kind again, yet, inside her, her own
clutch
of offspring are waiting to be born. And among them,
an unlikely prince will rise to become the future leader
of their kind. CLARIA!

~

The Captain will not remember that in the
subterfuge of time and space, he will
slither among the immortals, reborn into
the spirit of a demon fish!

~

Outlaw Poets

Beneath a whistling breeze, outlaw
poets
start to gather. Bedonia has a
fondness for drinking blood and
fire dancing. She's good at sustaining
a large enough flame to create the
visual effects. Rings of fire, like the flaming
hands of Hades, spin, in wistful sights,
highlighting the red of her hair.
Silas has an affinity for wormholes,
and travels portals of other dimensions
and parallel universes. He speaks of
vortexes and other worldly events while
he appears and reappears, then vanishing
without a trace. Mekia is from
Bimini and is into teleportation. She
often speaks of an electronic fog
and how she travelled 100 miles in 3 minutes.
Kiki is from an alien species that lives
underwater. Electromagnetic fields
recently caused a 9.2 magnitude earthquake
creating anomalies and vortices that changed
the DNA of her people.
Within the shrubs and plants,

within the thicket of high
trees waving in the breeze,
they walk together, spilling
their words as their energy
sweeps, born of both wonder
and terror alike,
shooting up through air,
streamlining the horizon.
Detestable curses and spells
for protection shatter the dome
over the material screen,
invading souls, even those lost
and forgotten, with fire,
highlighting auras, calling on
phantoms with pallid skin.
Blue moonlight surrounds them,
incubating them with its power
while banshees scream spitting
blood into the four corners of the
universe. Your time is numbered
no matter where you are, where you're from,
no matter who you are. The wraiths of
time know the hour of our demise and they
coil themselves around us until we fall
transparent,
into a cold,
dead,
stare,
yet,
the words live on.

Birds twitter,
reinforcing the tapestry of vocal
expression. Even unspoken words,
ache to explode within the silence
of death and often do
as time ultimately tells their story.
They are immortals, you know,
the outlaw poets, the writers,
the artists,
who move fast and steady
through gloomy clouds
formed by the collective
consciousness,
that ties us all together.

~

THE IMMORTALS

Do you hear us?
Our souls canvas the forest,
like an erotic flame that
works its way into the natural
world,
an extension of nature and
magic
that never fades away.
We are a clan with shared
stories, dimensions,
seeking
a
breath
back to a
human form.
We carry our swords
our shields,
our hopes, dreams and
sorrows,
obliterated by the greed
of mankind.
And yet, we are
bequeathed to this place,
to one another,
where Truth becomes a
formal presence,

in The Kingdom of
Our Savior.
We are the signs of beauty
canvassed by the grandeur
of night,
a crescendo of stars,
of ageless light
within the darkness
of a
maelstrom.

~

Two ships pass one another in
the darkness of a moonless night.
On land there is a uneasy feeling,
among hypnotic eyes
transfixed in the sky. Nothingness
fortifies the place, the mood, like a
silent promise of something coming,
embracing the solitude of sacred
moments. Double paths seem to
entwine before eyes trailing an
empty
blank space.
Inside a small house,
near a lake, a crystal chandelier
shimmers among the subtle glow of
candles, ritually arranged over a
magnificent altar to the Hindu goddess

Lakshmi and the great god, Vishnu.
There a poet dreams and pens a story
about
nothing existing anywhere, in the falsehood
of life where two ships sail beyond and away
from one another, remaining calm between
the absurdity of life, without the knowledge
 of the moon or the stars in the universe to
help guide the way.

~

To the reader.
You are trapped.
You are boxed in.

No one will be able,
to pinpoint your
destination.

~

Navigation has halted.
You are lost...

~

Outlaw poets steal souls.
They keep them, saving
them for a rainy day.

In the architect of dreams,
outlaw poets seek to destroy
the new ways, implementing
the ways of olde. They will
not implicate themselves,
they will not let you enquire.
Within the astronomy of space
that moves rapidly across
the irregularities of certain
and sure miracles, lights
flicker through hidden reservoirs,
that hold the remains of potent
magic, not as a punishment nor
as a blessing, but as a promise,
for the wonder that is to come.

~

My dear reader, you are celled.
Your future is ill-fated.
You are celled.

~

Outlaw poets speak of a last
dynasty, one that will rule
like a mercenary, silencing
voices, watching like a warden
in a prison for any little infraction,
polluting the free spirits, tying

their will, penalizing their
creativity.

~

Outlaw Poets will not be trapped.
Outlaw Poets will not be celled.
They will roam the outer banks
of dark space, screaming vehement
curses to the winds that carry them
in rebellion.

~

Outlaw Poets are the resistance.

~

Outlaw Poets spin around you,
around me. Their sling is David's,
deeply embedded into the mystical
stones and occult sketches of
the universe.

~

They will tell your story.

~

There's a one eyed poet,
spying on you.

~

A gunshot goes off,
a repeated pattern,
a residual energy,
that lowers
the temperature
with a sultry
chill.
The sound,
stretching,
prolonging
the seconds,
into
the
large
expanse
of
time.

~

There's a man
talking about a
woman's tits

as he escorts
her to his car.
Her yell is
quiet,
a whisper,
among the
loneliness
of
abuse.
The Captain
Is
Dead.
But there are others,
never-ending
others,
herding women
toward
terrible
horrific
exits.

~

Stay on guard.

~

The Spiritist is within you.

~

She is your intuition,
your healer,
your traditions.

~

Reclaim her!

~

Come into your power.

~

Free yourself.

Cuba and the Yoruba Pantheon

The natives are harvesting organs,
throwing the remains of the bodies
into the open space of the Cauto
River. A prelude to the spiritual
offerings that are entombed in
ghostly winds that carry the sprays
of the water like a priest's blessing.
Dark folklore bridges the windswept
droplets, summoning the spirits that
crave to possess, salivating over
those grounded, besieged by the
moon. Silvery showers of misty
rain, untamed and raw, highlight
the primordial lust between a man
and a woman, a sublime union of
chaotic
mysticism.
There's a sudden rise to the
corporeal apex summoning
ancient gods among witches
bestowed of fame by the sea.
Wild euphoria in the labyrinth
of the night, impassioned by
power, bleeds sensuous rituals
born of sacrifice, under the coven

of Yemaya.
Primal bedrock sets the narratives
of occultism hidden secretly
in people's devotions to the white
saints of the Spanish colonists.
Spiritists cast their hands over
flowing waters protected by
towering trees, adamant to satisfy
roots with the drink of dark
sustenance. In this state of
existence, Olodumare provides
the breath of life in a beautiful
proclamation of love, where
witches and practitioners, drum
and sing scared incantations
among herbs, amulets and charms,
to the divining powers of the
four winds.

~

Regla de Ocha and Regla
Lucumi pay homage to
Olofi, the divine essence
of all that exists. The
overarching divinity,
the creator of all beings,
who dwells among us.
There are forbidden
doorways, caminos

or roads of different
manifestations that
only Elegua can
open for he is the
guardian of the
crossroads and
thresholds, the messenger
between humanity
and the orishas.
He releases the grip,
but for a second, opening
your destiny to portal and
travel allowing all creatures
to return home,
momentarily. Those who
speak his name are aware
of the sacred bloodline,
the sacred omniscience
which connect us to our
ancestors,
to everything.
Energy and symbolism
alike bear spiritual fruit,
by way of magic and olde
traditions while cowrie
shells guard and protect
against all evil.

~

A burial took place today in
Havana. A military chief
rested under the watchful
gaze of Ogun, while in the
Sierra Maestra near the
province of Oriente,
a Babalawo or high priest
prepares silver pieces,
fruit and rum as an offering
while Ochosi watches silently
from the woods. There is a
sulfur smell that permeates
the grounds, surely it is
a warning from Osun
that something evil comes
this way. The Babalawo
takes notice, heeds the warning,
before running back to his
sanctuary in the old,
Oriente province.

~

By the river, where an
elderly man and his dog
live, daily rituals take
place in honor of Yemaya,
Ochun, Oya, Chango,
Obatala, Babalu Aye,
And Orula. Music plays

observing the mystical
beauty of the land,
as wind, lightening, death,
sacrifice and fire, ignite
the pantheon, the divine
force.
Ache'

~

A dark witch lags around
a large garden statue. The
roof of her house symbolically
spans many directions,
rustic in appearance
and geometry,
it traditionally holds
many secrets.
Orchids peek out in
curiosity, for she is
young, sophisticated,
beautiful. Mangos off
surrounding trees make
a hearty snack. She travels
the night in a trance-like
state, as stars begin to
sparkle as if they were
birthing newly into
radiance. She is born
and bred of Palo

Mayombe, and
she can hurt as much as
she can heal. Her ancestors,
Central African people
from the Congo Basin,
enslaved in Cuba many
moons ago. Wooden
sticks prepare her altars,
stacked in place by a
sacred cauldron as she
works directly with the
muertos, with the dead.
People come from far
off places, all over Cuba
all over the world to see
her, wearing white head
coverings as a sign of
respect.
And through the milky-colored
vortexes of both space and
time, seers, travellers,
demons, angels, ancestral
spirits, deities, nature sprites,
fairies and alien nations, watch
and study, before briskly
disappearing into oblivion.

~

In the Basilica Santuario
Nacional De La Caridad
Del Cobre, the roman
catholic church of
Our Lady of Charity,
a priest prepares the altar
for daily mass. It sits in
the village of El Cobre,
about 12 miles west of
Santiago de Cuba. The
bell tower is red, crowed
by two side towers of the
same color. Often, the
believers would have to
take cover and hide from
Padre Simon, who loved
to make his way to the
bell tower every afternoon
after getting drunk on
communion wine. He
would take pot shots with
his rifle in hand at anything that
moved in his vicinity,
often revealing all told
to him in the sanctity of
confession. And every
afternoon, his brother,
Lucio, the local Babalawo
or high priest, called out
to him, avoiding the flying

bullets, begging him
to come down from the
bell tower, before he
killed someone. You
could set your watch
by Simon's responses.
He would continue
shooting, ringing the bell,
and yelling back at his
brother that he was a
demon sent by the devil
himself to corrupt his
pure soul. Lucio
always managed to scold
him down from the
bell tower after Simon
exhausted himself with
threats and gunfire. And
even though the parishioners
witnessed the spectacle,
every afternoon for years,
they still went to confession,
lighting a candle to
Our Lady of Charity that
Padre Simon would adhere
to the sacred seal of
confession.

~

Santeros sacrificed a goat.
They slit its throat, let the
blood gush forth, catching
it a cast iron basin,
offered to the creator deity,
Olodumare.
A spiritual doll is given to
a child.
A spirit,
trapped,
attached,
within the doll,
must do her bidding.
Must protect
her,
at all costs.

The doll
cries,
real
tears.

~

Its spirit is
trapped.
Celled.

~

Elegua comes forth
to bless the child
of his own.
She will have
the
gift.

~

In a nearby mountain
by a cave shaft,
a white witch consumes
a bottle of rum. Her
vocabulary is not
of this world.
There's a string of
Knots under her
fingertips.
She's building
a grotto
to Yemaya,
as cascades
of
sacred
water,
fall
calmly
into
sacrifice.
She blesses

herself,
as she
drinks,
solidifying
her identity
as
a
White
Witch.

~

In el barrio Chino
in Havana, an
old woman is
practicing
Feng Shui.
She wants to slow
the energy
flow of
her house.
On the sparsely
furnished
living room,
a magic
square
holds
incense.
She pauses,
seeking

balance
from
the
five
elements,
keeping
the
path
to
the
front
door
clear.

~

Oddities
Spin
Around
Us.

~

You the reader,
are celled.

~

You are the
protagonists,

of this
construction.

~

You are the
recording,
the
instrument,
held
within
my
photographic
image
of
the
universe.

~

Dark

~

Cold

~

Nature

~

Shifts

~

Changes

Even

~

The

~

Light

~

Alters

~

You

~

Are

~

Physically

~

Acted

~

Upon

~

You

~

Are

~

Trapped

Rum Runners and Pirate Saints

Footsteps plague the scene;
two sets, one double the size
of the other, pressed hard into
sand.
The silent siren of death recruits
the moon, and it complies as if
overwhelmed by helplessness,
in its Gibbous phase.
Mutilated bodies contort in agony
while blood fills the beach without
the vision of a sunken chest to
ease the pain;
surely, the devil was in their midst
and the fervent bottles of rum would
not serve as appeasement either,
but will possess them in evil instead.
In the distance, a drummer plays
to the beat of the Orishas, but the
houses along the coastline are dark
and still.
The echoes of their screams have
stopped in unison with the dead,
fading off into the blues of the night
sky.
As for the two footprints, only

a day will pass. One day, in the
labyrinth of life where your future
can be foretold for only ten dollars.
One day, where the mysteries
of the universe can become a
flourishing business, in a land of kill
or be killed.

~

The reincarnation of the captain and the spiritist.

The moon shines over the Cuban
province of Matanzas with a narcissistic
vulnerability that makes even the tourists
take notice. These encapsulated moments
of insight are viewed as spiritual
communication from the Orishas
themselves, especially when they take place
during one of the initiation ceremonies.
Lanterns swing on and off in the far rolling hills
north of the province as the sand clatters
across stone and rock in the beach resort of
Varadero, where the martial beat of pounding
drums increase in intensity with the crashing
waves and ocean surges that rip away layers
of sediment under the surface.
To the south, by the swamp lands and the beach
of Giron, a disorienting mist is forming into an

ominous cloud, blocking out the moon as it billows
empty from its place of execution. The wildlife
loom their heads in its direction, almost as if they
anticipate its arrival.

The long stretch of fertile plains in central Matanzas
smells of tobacco, citrus fruits, and sugar, a repeated
scent that remains attached to the air, carried by the
wind into the skin, hair and lungs of every living
inhabitant of the island. Even the post mortem damage
to the skeletonized corpse of an unidentified animal,
doesn't inhibit that sweet smell.

By a secluded beach in Guama, home of one of the
largest underground cave and lake systems in
Latin America, santeros dressed in blue and white
garments with silver trimmings pay homage to
Yemaya
in a series of musical prayers called bembe. The
instrumental rhythms fill the igbodu', the ceremonial
space, begging for the throne, the seat of the Orishas.
Ritual blue and white beads adorn the necks of the
participants and a cloth canopy of the same colors
drape the vessel to the secrets of the Orisha. Heads
tilt back, floating as though no body were attached,
keep time with the Lucumi tunes. Some of the dancers
lose their balance and tumble, a clear indication
the Orishas are near.

The oru' cantado or sung oration calls on them:
Elegua, Oya', Ogun, Yemaya', Obtala', Ochun,
and Chango'. A black rooster is snatched by its neck
and offered as sacrifice. Rosario gives an anguished

cry of protest as a new contraction grips at her very soul.

Soon she will give birth.

Blood streaked thighs are fully exposed as her face contorts in pain; the flames of the bonfire, overturn the darkness, rekindling the night with magic. At first Rosario doesn't feel the baby move down, but she feels the crowning. One more push and she will be born. The rumble of drums, chants and dancing seems to incite

strong winds that spray the heaving earth with salt water,

as if by command.

The circle dancing around Rosario

becomes more violent, spinning, gliding closer to her and her unborn child. One of the santeras, her sister, Maria, is mounted by the Orisha Yemaya and begins to speak as the vessel for the ritual possession. In tongue, she thanks her children for the banana chips and pork cracklings left as offering, the rum, black-eyed peas, sugar cane molasses and watermelon. Rosario's head flails from side to side and she lays panting as her screams

reduce her to exhaustion.

Maria, still in ritual possession, touches Rosario's stomach.

A burst of red splatters the sand beneath her, and then the wailing of a baby.

"Baby Alicia! Child of my heart, child of the sea!" Maria says,

and she looks over at Escobar before collapsing to the
ground.
Carlos holds his newborn baby girl in his arms before
he wraps
her up in a blanket and hands her to her mother.
Rosario looks
down to see bluish skin streaked with blood as the
now rising
sun puts an end to the night's chill.
Gale force winds and water start to inundate roads,
billowing
violently over bridges, pervading the Valley of Vinales
as if
summoned to complete a specific task. There are
murmurs
muttered in exasperation, desperate hands gathered
around
a half a dozen breeding tanks occupying the lush
gardens
of a government-funded estate. The water levels in the
pools
rise faster, and the quest to drain them becomes like a
puzzle
or twisted game.
Brackish water continues to slosh over its edges,
overflowing
onto the cobblestone walkways that are littered with
glossy
green leaves and orange blossoms. First glance at the
nearest

breeding tank, surrounded by purple jacaranda,
creates panic.
The Claria are escaping. Their unique form of
locomotion
is unmistakable. With a preternatural sense they head
for the
jungle that borders the property… for the river system
that lays
beyond.
Only those involved will bless themselves and Cuba
against
the terror the hurricane has just unleashed. Only those
involved will appreciate this very personal message,
from
Mother Nature herself!
Debris falls in a courtyard as the sky turns an ominous
red-pink. Baby Alicia, lying in her crib, seems
delighted
by all the activity. Rosario could almost swear she sees
Alicia's blanket ripple a bit even though the room is
secure
from any breeze. And Alicia, with wide grin, arms
spread
apart, flailing, seems to be responding to Mother
Nature's
precarious spectacle, with welcoming arms.
The next day the sun is shining like an oracle
in the sky. Fingers of intermittent light follow
movement,
penetrating the depths of murky waters. In the

shallows
where the lilies are thick, a female Claria sloshes about
like
a serpent, looking for food. The sky settles down on the
earth as the clouds dissipate in heated air. All is calm.
Loneliness does not fail to induced a rush of hormones
that fuels her hunger. A burst of speed, jaws open,
a brief struggle; the end of a silvery tilapia's life. And
in the shallows, amid the vegetation, a clutch of tilapia
eggs meet the same fate. She dines on them like the
queen that she is.
Loneliness.
Her family is scattered throughout the myriad
of waterways that lace the countryside. She longs to be
with her own kind again, yet, inside her, her own
clutch
of offspring are waiting to be born. And among them,
an unlikely prince will rise to become the future leader
of their kind. CLARIA!

To be continued…

You

Are

Free

ABOUT THE AUTHOR

I write from the heart. If I don't feel it, I can't write it. And there's always a spiritual element found in my writings. All of them. I'm a real person just like you, and we're (all writers, artists and poets) probably more alike than we are different regardless of race, color, philosophy. That's my emotional truth and I hope that comes out in all my work. I also believe the worst thing a writer can do is overthink — just feel and go with that. If it's done right, it should be like you're channeling and tapping into something greater and outside yourself, even though in all reality it is coming from within.

www.ingramcontent.com/pod-product-compliance
Lightning Source LLC
Chambersburg PA
CBHW060955050726
47592CB00003B/1232